Divriği Castle Excavation
2006 - 2018

Erdal Eser & Meryem Acara Eser

Copyright © 2023 E. Eser–M. Acara Eser

All rights reserved.

ISBN: 9798858016588

Imprint: Independently published

Names: Eser, Erdal, author. | Acara Eser, Meryem, author. | Belgin Selen Haktanır, translator. | Ivana Mihaljinec, translator and editor.

Title: Divriği Castle Excavation 2006-2018 / edited by Ivana Mihaljinec

Author photographs by Erdal Eser and Meryem Acara Eser

Cover design by Ivana Mihaljinec

DEDICATION

To all who have worked with or without sound…

Editor's note

This book is a cross-section of 12 years of hard work. As Prof.dr. Erdal Eser was Head of the Divrigi Castle excavation and Assoc. Prof. Meryem Acara Eser co-leader of the excavation and restoration project, along with the team consisted of professionals in specific field and archaeology and art history students, this book gives us a detailed insight of how the castle and its "secret chambers" had been revealed through the years. Invaluable are thousands of findings, in this book presented only a few. The field survey which had been conducted has revealed some precious gems like 2 inscriptions found at the Main Gate, the hamam, the Sultan's Gate and some well preserved metal, ceramic, bone and glass objects and bracelets. Hundreds of pieces of pottery reveal the craftmanship of Late Roman-Byzantine and Seljuk period, with some unique examples found at Divriği Castle. Altogether 3576 pieces are recorded in the inventory of the excavation, and this research is still ongoing under the supervision of the authors.

Although the active excavation seized in 2018, and the restoration of the castle walls has been almost finished, there is still more to be unearthed and found. This book shows how the work has been done and offers a firm ground for the future exploration and research of this amazing area and the castle itself.

Ivana Mihaljinec
August 2023

CONTENTS

1	Introduction	8
2	Divriği Castle	11
3	Excavation seasons	19
4	Field introduction	46
5	Finds	83
6	Evaluation	113
7	Closing remarks	121
8	About the authors	123

1 INTRODUCTION

Rich mineral deposits and Paulicians activity were the reason for recognition of Divriği by the Turks who were coming to Anatolia after its fall in the hands of Mengüjeks. There is not enough data available about Mengüjek activities in this settlement. As an important source from which we can learn are the mosque and the underground spaces inside the Castle area. The excavation works on the Divriği Castle started in 2007. In the initial years, the working area was known under the name Upper Church [Yukarı Kilise]. The cleaning process of a building from 1268/1851-52 was carried out. On the inside of the wall, the excavation in 2009 revealed a place that seems to be a workshop venue. In 2010, excavations inside the castle continued along the West wall with the aim of finding an entry point into the castle and opening of the Main Gate and Sultan's Gate begun. From this year on, it seemed necessary to do the excavation and cleaning work in that area inside the wall. The little book in your hands contains a general introduction on the excavation works that have been done in 2006-2018 period.

Between 2006-2018, the following works have been finished: rubble stone lattice and mortar soil were annexes from later periods, especially in the lower area where the bath houses are situated, and in the Lower Castle part the second masjid was built. These are some of the conclusions that were made. In these areas, drywall decoration, glazed and unglazed parts of vessels, parts of glass bracelets, metal and various processed bone objects were found. The finds mostly belong to the 12th century and later periods.

In recent years, the restoration of the city walls has begun. Our wish is that upon the successful completion of the wall restoration, the landscape project be implemented as soon as possible.

E. Eser-M. Acara Eser
Divriği, 2018

2 DIVRİĞİ CASTLE

Divriği Castle, the first construction of which is thought to be in the Byzantine period, constitutes one of the important examples of the Middle Ages Anatolian-Turkish Military Architecture. The building, that has survived to the present day with its establishment in harmony with the topographical conditions of the area in which it is located, has been the subject of a limited number of studies. Most of this research are about Castle Mosque.

The castles, together with the examples remaining in the settlement, are important especially because the old settlement pattern is preserved within the walls. Divriği Castle also draws attention because it reflects these features.

An archaeological excavation in Divriği Castle is necessary to reveal the settlement pattern. While doing this, the known historical perspective of the Mengujeks will be examined in detail.

It is thought that the new data to be presented in the national and international scientific platforms will make important contributions to the Mengujeks and the history of the region.

Location-Geographical Structure

Divriği is located in the southeast of Sivas, near the Central Anatolian border of the Upper Euphrates section of the Eastern Anatolia Region, at an altitude of 1250 meters from the sea, on the valley floor and slopes of the stream that joins with the Çaltı river, one of the branches of the Euphrates. The first place where the city was founded is the castle vicinity and its skirts, who are located on a hill descending to the Çaltı valley with very steep slopes in the northeastern part.[1] Due to the fact that the settlement is surrounded by high mountains, difficulties are encountered in transportation. External connection of the district is provided by Sivas-Erzincan railway and Sivas-Divriği highway. Sivas is 179 km by railway and 184 km by road. It is surrounded by Erzincan in the east, Kangal in the west, Zara and İmranlı in the north, and Malatya in the south.[2]

---

[1] A. Balgalmış, "Divriği", *TDV İslâm Ansiklopedisi*, 9, İstanbul 1994, pp. 452-454, esp. p. 452.

[2] H. Denizli, *Sivas Tarihi ve Anıtları*, Sivas 1995, p. 225; "Divriği is the district center of Sivas province. It is on the banks of the Çaltı Suyu, a tributary of the Euphrates, and its name actually reflects this topography. The historical name of the town was used especially in the form of Tephrike in the Byzantine era. Since we encounter variations such as Abra, Abphra, Ebra, and İbra of the Anatolian word meaning "plenty of water, abundant water", we can see that the ephr[a] part called Tephrike reflects one of those variations. The name of the same settlement was used in Arabic sources in the form of Aprike; there is also a variation of your name in the Armenian dialect called Aprig, that is, Apr[a]-ig, whose initial D- is omitted." B. Umar, *Türkiye'deki Tarihsel Adlar*, İstanbul 1993, p. 218.

The outer wall length of the castle, which is located in the north-south direction and on a high hill, reaches 1.500 meters with the destroyed walls of the inner castle. Its north-south span is 400 meters, and its east-west width is approximately 200 meters. There are bastions along the walls surrounding the Outer and Inner Castle; it has a square, polygonal and circular plan. Outer Castle walls open to the city with two gates located in the southwest and west, but the first gate was built later and the second was destroyed except for its arch. The height of the eastern walls varies between 5-8 meters and the walls have a seating plan suitable for topographical conditions.[3]

---

[3] H. Denizli, *ibid.*, p. 227.

General History

Historical information about Divriği begins with the scene of the Sassanid-Byzantine struggle (Photo 1).

Photo 1- Divriği Castle, Aerial View

After the Sassanids withdrew from the stage of history, Arab-Byzantine conflicts began in the region. III. As a result of the Anatolian campaign of Mikhail in the middle of the 9th century, Divriği fell into the hands of the Byzantine forces.[4] Although there is Byzantine domination in the region, Divriği is the center of the Paulicians. It is not known exactly how long the dominance of the Paulicians in Divriği continued, which from time to time sided with different powers.[5]

It is not known when the definitive Turkish domination in the region and in Divriği began. However, it is considered that it was captured by Mengüjek Gazi or his sons in the years following the Battle of Manzikert in 1071.[6]

In 1142, after the disintegration of the Mengüjek State, Divriği, which fell to the share of Mengüjek Süleyman Shah, became the capital of the Divriği branch of the Mengüjeks. Divriği, that was under the dominance of the Anatolian Seljuk State in the second quarter of the 13th century, could not resist the Mongol pressure in the days following the Kösedağ War in

---

[4] F. Işıltan, *Bizans Devleti Tarihi*, Ankara 1981, pp. 212-220.
[5] O. Turan, *Doğu Anadolu'da Türk Devletleri Tarihi*, İstanbul 1981, p. 55; There is a castle settlement in Divrigi at this time.
[6] O. Turan, *ibid.*, p. 55; N. Sakaoğlu, *Türk Anadolu'da Mengücekoğulları*, İstanbul 1971, p. 597; G. Eken, *Fiziki, Sosyal ve İktisâdî Açıdan Divriği, [1775-1845]*, A.Ü. Sos. Bil. Ens. Tarih Anabilim Dalı, Yayımlanmamış Doktora Tezi, Ankara 1993, p. 1.

1243.[7] In 676 [1277], the Mongolian ruler Abaka, who came to this country due to the Anatolian campaign of the Mamluk sultan Baybars, stopped by Divriği and ordered the walls to be demolished.[8]

There is not much information about the history of Divriği from the beginning of the 14th century until the end of the 14th century. Although Sivas was subject to the Ilkhanids and then the Eretnids in this century, Divriği was in the hands of the Mamluks. Meanwhile, Divriği, joined with the Ottoman lands during the campaigns of Yıldırım Bayezid in the region at the end of the 14th century, was again left to the Mamluks with the alliance made with the Mamluks due to the approaching Timur threat. Divriği was definitely under Ottoman rule only after the Mercidabik victory [1516].[9]

Research History

Since Divriği entered literature mostly with its social complex, studies on the castle are limited. Although there have been studies on the Castle Mosque in recent years, there is no

---

[7] O. Turan, *ibid.*, p. 60.
[8] O. Turan, *ibid.*, p. 62; N. Sakaoğlu, *ibid.*, p. 75; F. Sümer, "Mengücekler", *İslâm Ansiklopedisi*, 7, Eskişehir 1997, p. 713-718, know. p. 717. Although it is not known whether this order was carried out, it is highly probable that the gate in the southwest corner was canceled during this period.
[9] G. Eken, *ibid,* p. 2.

detailed study or research about the Castle, which is an important example of military architecture.

Like many other settlements in Anatolia, the first information about Divriği and its Castle is obtained from the books written by historians and travelers.[10]

---

[10] Some of the researches containing information about Divriği are as follows; Strabon, *Geographica/Coğrafya*, XII/I,II,III, [trans. A.Pekman], İÜ.Ed.Fak, Istanbul 1969, XII, 8; Kâtip Çelebi, *Cihannüma*, Müteferrika Tabı, İstanbul [1145/1729], pp. 624-625; W.F. Ainsworth, *Travels and Researches in Asia Minor, Mesopotamia, Chaldes and Armenia*, II, Londra 1842, p. 8; M. V. de Saint-Martin, *Description Historique et Geographique de L'Asie Mineure*, II, Paris 1852, pp. 577-578; C. Ritter, "Divrigi", *Die Erdkunde*, X, Berlin 1859, pp. 795-799, esp. pp.795-797; V. Cuinet, *La Turqui d'Asie, Geographie administrative statistique descriptive Et raisonne de chanque province de L'Asie-Mineure*, I, Paris 1892, pp. 687-688; M.F. Grenard, "Notes Sur les Monuments du Moyen âge Malatia, Divrighi, Siwas, Darendeh, Amasia et Tokat", *Societe Asiatique*, XVII, Paris 1891, pp. 549-553, esp. pp. 554-555; Şemseddin Sami , *Kamusu'l Âlam, Tarih ve Coğrafya Lügâti*, III, Mihran Matbaası, İstanbul 1892, p. 2220; V.W. Yorke, "A Journey in the Valley of the Upper Euphrates", *Geographical Journal*, VIII, 1896, p. 453; Evliya Çelebi, *Seyahatname*, II-III, İkdam Matbaası, Dersaadet 1898, pp. 211-214; M. van Berchem, *Materiaux Pour Des Corpus Inscriptionum Arabicarum*, Le Caire 1910, III, pl. 5; A.D. Mordtmann, *Anatolien, Skizzen und Reisebriefe aus Kleinasien [1850-1859]*, Hannover 1925, p. 442; A. Gabriel, *Monuments Turcs d'Anatolie*, II, Paris 1934; A.S. Ülgen, "Divriği'nin Şehircilik ve Anıtları Yönünden İncelenmesi", *Mimarlık*, 5/6, Ankara 1948, pp. 33-37; W. M. Ramsay, *Anadolu'nun Tarihi Coğrafyası*, [Çev. M. Pektaş], M. E. Basımevi, İstanbul 1961; Önge ve diğerleri , *Divriği Ulu Camii ve Darüşşifası*, Vakıflar Genel Müdürlüğü Yayınları, Ankara 1978; A. Durukan ve M. S. Ünal, *Anadolu Selçuklu Dönemi Sanatı Bibliyografyası*, Atatürk Kültür Merkezi Yayını, Ankara 1994; Sakaoğlu, *Türk Anadolu'da Mengücekoğulları*, Yapı Kredi Yayınları, İstanbul 2005, pp. 189-238.

When the aforementioned studies are examined, although the castle is on a rocky hill and its first construction dates to the Paulician period, it is in fact a medieval castle with its general appearance and material-technical features. The existence of two castle gates, one of which was closed later, and the presence of some building remains, warehouses and arsenals along the wall, indicate that there are remains of a Melik Pavilion [palace], an Ahmedek, supported with the inscriptions and figurative decorations on the walls. In addition, according to Evliya Çelebi, who visited Divriği in 1649, there are records of rainwater cisterns, wheat warehouses, ammunition, 300 earth-roofed houses, a mosque and two gates in the castle.[11]

---

[11] N. Sakaoğlu, *ibid.*, p. 209.

3 EXCAVATION SEASONS

2006-2009

Studies on Divriği Castle started with the survey conducted in 2006.[12] In the related research, the situation of the area was determined by wandering around the castle and its surroundings. In the same year, an application to initiate the excavation was made to the Ministry of Culture and Tourism. In 2007, the study gained the status of the Council of Ministers Decisive Excavation.[13]

In the same year, the Castle Mosque was included in the repair program by the Sivas Regional Directorate of Foundations.[14] We found it appropriate to work outside the city walls in the first year of the excavation due to the cable car

---

[12] E. Eser, M. Acara Eser, "Divriği Kalesi Yüzey Araştırması 2006", *25. Uluslararası Kazı, Araştırma ve Arkeometri Sempozyumu, 28 May-1 June 2007, Kocaeli,* Ankara 2008, pp. 247-256.

[13] E. Eser, "Divriği Kalesi 2007", C.Ü. Sosyal Bilimler Dergisi, 34/1, May 2009, pp. 38-42 [Excavation Report].

[14] The cleaning and documentation of the interior and exterior of the building before the repair was answered negatively by the Regional Directorate of Foundations.

built for material transportation and the electricity-water line laid in places. For this reason, the cleaning work of the structure known as the Upper Church among the public has been started (Photo 2).[15]

Photo 2- Upper Church, General View, 2007

---

[15] There are various stories about the demolition of the building, which is located in the First-Degree Archaeological Site. Despite its dilapidated appearance and being inside the district, it still attracts the attention of illegal excavation enthusiasts.

The cleaning of the rubble inside the Upper Church continued during three excavation seasons covering the years 2007-2009 (Photo 3).

Photo 3- Upper Church, After Cleaning, General View

In 2009, while the cleaning of the church was continuing, it was decided to carry out a verification study on the geophysical studies that had been done before. As a result of the studies carried out in the section to the west of the Castle

Mosque, which we call the 2009 trench, the space group, noticed as a result of geophysical surveys and thought to be a workshop, was unearthed (Photo 4).[16]

Photo 4- 2009 Trench, General View

---

[16] A. Büyüksaraç, E. Eser, Ö. Bektaş, A. B. Akay, S. Koşaroğlu, "Surface Geophysical Investigations and Preliminary Excavation at Divrigi Citadel" *Mediterranean Archaeology&Archaeometry*, 12/2, 2012, pp. 129-138.

2010

2010 is the season when the works inside the walls started. The works at Main Gate and Sultan's Gate started this season (Photo 5-6).[17] The reason for starting work on both gates is the desire to remove the rubble waste to be formed and to continue the excavation by following the ground by finding a possible solid ground. Unsurprisingly, the gates were not easy to open. Removing the thick fill layer created by both the in-situ and flowing debris necessitated great efforts to be made by the team.[18]

---

[17] E. Eser, A. B. Akay, "Divriği Kalesi: 2010", *33. Uluslararası Kazı, Araştırma ve Arkeometri Sempozyumu, 23-28 May 2011, Malatya*, 4, Ankara 2012, pp.437-446.

[18] Excavation in or near the settlement brings various difficulties. First of all, it is not easy to remove the rubble from the area due to the existing human and vehicle traffic. For this reason and to prevent uncontrolled entrances from the ruined parts of the wall, it was decided to drain the rubble out. The resulting image is disturbing, but it has been successful in terms of controlling the area. At the end of the excavations, all rubble piles will be removed from the site and its surroundings.

Photo 5- Main Gate, Before Excavation, General View

Photo 6- Sultan's Gate, Before Excavation, General View

2011[19]

In 2011, in addition to the previous works, the Anonymous Structure and the Flag Zone started to be opened (Photo 7).[20]

Photo 7- Anonymous Structure, Before Excavation, General View

---

[19] E. Eser, "Divriği Kalesi: 2011", *34. Uluslararası Kazı, Araştırma ve Arkeometri Sempozyumu, 28 May-01 June 2012, Çorum*, Ankara 2013, pp. 415-426.

[20] The fact that the Castle Mosque is in this region causes the surrounding area to be excavated for various reasons during the works for the mosque, such as laying electrical wiring or erecting poles. In order to prevent this destruction, excavation decision was taken in this region. As will be stated in the detailed introductions of the fields, the studies carried out in this section have led to important findings.

The structure is called Anonymous, since we do not yet understand its function; it probably has a storage function.[21] Although its floor has been reached, there is no data about its entrance yet (Photo 8).[22]

Photo 8- Anonymous Structure, After Excavation, General View

---

[21] It is also said that there is a pool. However, this does not seem possible.
[22] It is certain that there will be more information on this subject when it is opened.

2012[23]

In 2012, in addition to the works started and carried out in previous years, the construction of the terracing to the east of the Main Gate was started. It has been decided to make terracing in the slope areas where the slope reaches 70% in places. The presence of the gate played a role in the selection of the area.[24] One of the results reached during these studies was that there may be some houses with their own private baths in the area (Photo 9).

Photo 9- East of the Main Gate, Residence with Bath

---

[23] E. Eser, "Divriği Kalesi: 2012", *35. Uluslararası Kazı, Araştırma ve Arkeometri Sempozyumu, 27-31 May 2013, Muğla,* Ankara 2014, pp. 155-177.

[24] It is aimed to protect the gate area from the current and to reduce the load on this section. Thus, it was possible to understand the construction method realized in this section.

Another work started this season is the opening of a road that will connect the castle and the Great Mosque. For the road, which has a width of 2.00 meters in places, the concrete water channel built by the Municipality of Divriği was used as the ground. The roads that were opened and planned to be expanded in the future will be used both for opening the bottom of the city wall and for removing the accumulated rubble.

2013[25]

During the 2013 excavation season, the section we call the 3rd Bastion, located to the north of the Main Gate, was added to the known areas (Photo 10).

Photo 10- Three Zodiac Signs, Before Excavation, General View

---

[25] E. Eser, M. Görür, "Divriği Kalesi: 2013", *36. Uluslararası Kazı, Araştırma ve Arkeometri Sempozyumu, 02-06 June 2014, Gaziantep,* Ankara 2014, pp. 525-540.

It is aimed to gradually level the rough terrain of the inner walled section for the comfortable circulation of the visitors. At the end of this study, a second building, probably used as a residence, was found. It was understood from the opened spaces that it also had a private bath (Photo 11).

Photo 11- East of the Main Gate, Residence with Bath

One of the newly opened sections is the section we call the Cistern Area to the north of the Castle Mosque (Photo 12). The reason for the study here is the possibility of finding other cistern spaces next to the still visible and standing cistern.

In particular, it was desired to scan the area, that is very dangerous for visitors.[26]

Photo 12- Cistern Area, General View

---

[26] The warning sign we placed in this section was destroyed by unknown persons.

2014[27]

One of the new areas opened this season is the north of Castle Mosque (Photo 13).

Photo 13- North of Castle Mosque, General View

As it is known, the castle area is exposed to fires from time to time. It was decided to completely clean the surroundings of the Castle Mosque, so that it would not be damaged by fires. There is no longer a fire hazard, at least in this section, as the rock floor has been completely exposed.

---

[27] In the Art History Research Symposium held in Sivas in 2014, a general evaluation of the works carried out between 2006-2012 was presented. E. Eser, Divriği Kalesi Kazısı: 2006-2012", *XVI. Ortaçağ-Türk Dönemi Kazıları ve Sanat Tarihi Araştırmaları Sempozyumu Bildirileri, 18-20 October 2014/Proceedings of the Symposium of Medieval-Turkish Era Excavations and Art History Researches, 18-20th October 2012*, Cumhuriyet Üniversitesi Yayınları, Sivas 2014, pp. 405-420.

Divriği Castle is a double walled settlement. A very small part of the city wall dating to the Byzantine period can be seen today (Photo 14).

Photo 14- Inner Wall, Excavation Area, General View

The opening of the city wall is important in terms of restoration works. At least, a study was carried out in this section in order to find the location of the gate of the inner wall.

To the north of the area, there are two rock tomb chambers that are thought to have been used as a warehouse/housing function (Photo 15).

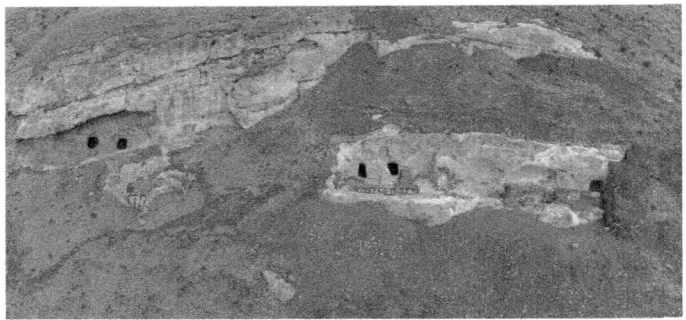

Photo 15- Rock Tomb Chambers, General View

The fact that the Divriği Castle is located on a rock promontory with a length of approximately 400 meters leads to the assessment that the number of rock spaces is higher. The details that emerged as a result of the studies carried out this season have verified this idea. This area will continue to be open.

Again, it was decided to clean the two-vaulted room in the south of the outer wall in order to assist the restoration work, which is thought to begin soon (Photo 16).

Photo 16- South Wall, Vaulted Units

The aforementioned section was repaired according to the results obtained after the cleaning activities.

2015

Studies are concentrated in the Sultan's Gate and Rock Cave Region. However, the cleaning of the structure known as the covered bazaar, located to the south of the main gate and to the north of the excavation house, has begun (Photo 17-18).[28]

---

[28] The ownership of the building belongs to the Municipality of Divriği. The places that are understood to have been used as warehouses, are in a neglected state today.

Photo 17- Covered Bazaar, Before Cleaning

Photo 18- Covered Bazaar, After Cleaning

2016

Work continued in the cave area. Although the working season is short, a group of stucco finds is very important.

It has been observed that a similar figural composition is found on a group of stuccos unearthed during the excavations in the cave area (Photo 19).

Photo 19- Stucco, Wall Cladding Board

Probably the pieces belonging to the same place were taken from where they were found and used as filling material. There are two different compositions on the pieces, a small part of which is combined. The first is from left to right: a hybrid creature with the body of a lion, wings and a bird's head; its lower body consists of a horse, the upper body of a human being shooting arrows, and finally a deer figure. The second composition is a sequence in which there is a goat [?] or a more harmless game animal on the front and there is a predator on the back side.

As can be understood from the fragments of the first composition, the same subject is given repeatedly on rectangular plaster boards of different sizes. In the middle [according to the viewer], within a circular frame formed by a thin inscription strip, there is a mixed creature whose lower body is in profile and to the left, and its upper body is turned to the right, holding a bow and arrow that it is about to throw, six horse-mounted human bodies and its tail ending in the shape of a dragon's head. To the right of this figure, there is a deer that looks to the right with its body turned to the left and its head turned back, which gives the impression that it is about to be hunted. It is understood from the stance of its front and hind legs that it is in motion. Unlike the central figure, there is no frame around it. The body of the third figure, located at the far left of the composition, looks to the right, while its head looks back to the left. It is a hybrid creature with a lion's body, a bird's head, wings, and its tail ends in a dragon's head like the central figure. There is no frame around it, as in the figure to the right of center. Both figures are bordered by inscription strips at the top and bottom. It is seen that the spaces outside the figures are filled with non-condensed vegetal motifs.

It is understood that the animals in the composition of the animal series, which is made in a thin strip, are in motion due to their posture. Their bodies are depicted in profile and running to the right. Their slender bodies end with a long and curled tail. Although the type of prey they chased at first cannot be clearly understood, it is an animal with long ears and a short tail. It is seen that simple vegetal filling, which is not dense, is applied to the cavities remaining from the bodies.

Sequences of various animals have been used in almost every culture. Hunting appears in itself as a royal act. It also symbolizes the dominance of the strong over the weak. The composition consisting of hybrid creatures actually depicts a hunting scene in its general form. The fact that the tails of the bird-headed creature that shoots an arrow and is behind it end with a dragon's head emphasizes being successful and strong the hunted animal. The creature, whose lower body is a horse and upper body is a human, holding bow and arrow, is known as Centaurus in astrology. The dragon is the symbol of Cevzahar, the eighth planet in Islamic mythology. Since Sagittarius is under the influence of the planet Cevzahar, it is normal for them to be seen together in most depictions. In this composition, the centaur, which symbolizes the Sultan, will most likely be successful in hunting, with hybrid creatures and dragons on their tails. The fact that the game animal is a deer suggests that the composition carries the meaning of abundance and fertility. A second possibility is that the person on whose behalf the decoration was made was born under the sign of Sagittarius. However, with our current knowledge, it is not possible to say anything definite about this issue.

The subject draws attention not only because of the pieces and the compositions on them, but also for another reason. It is also very important because of the article titled "The Cosmological Interpretation of the Stucco Piece in the Berlin Museum" by Ahmet Çaycı.[29]

The researcher comments in the related article: *"The stucco piece in the Berlin Museum is a work where fantastic and real creature meet on the same ground. The piece was taken from Anatolia [probably Konya] to the Berlin Museum. Its dimensions are 0.46x0.18 m and it is in a transverse rectangular form. The plastic work is made in the printing technique. There is no historical information on the piece. F. Sarre states that the mentioned work may belong to the 13th century. I would like to state that we can agree with the idea that the work may belong to the 13th century, based on the comparisons we have made with similar ones and the style critical data. The production center of the work is unknown. However, on this issue, F. Sarre puts forward two views. The first one is that the work may have been made in Konya by masters from the Southeast Anatolia region. And the second view is that it is possible that it may have been produced in Southeast Anatolia."*

---

[29] A. Çaycı, "Berlin Müzesi'ndeki Stuko Parçanın Kozmolojik Yorumu", *Ortaçağ'da Anadolu. Prof.Dr. Aynur Durukan'a Armağan*, H.Ü. Edebiyat Fakültesi Sanat Tarihi Bölümü Yayını, Ankara 2002, pp. 157-165.

Based on the pieces we have, it is possible to suggest that these pieces, which are very similar not only in composition but also in scale, were produced in Divriği. There is no doubt that the piece from Anatolia, whose place of origin is unknown, was taken from Divriği.

2017

The studies that had been started in the previous years in the cave area continued. Although it is expected that the stucco decoration pieces found during the previous season will continue, unfortunately no other pieces were found. In this section, an irregularly shaped space, the roof of which is supported by wooden pillars, was uncovered. It was observed that mud was used as binding material on the walls of the room built with rubble stone material and the floor was not leveled as in other similar room examples.

Another activity in the area was repair works. Plaster reinforcement works were carried out on all the walls of the place, which we call the Hammam Kiosk.

The works on the arrangement of the excavation depot and the documentation of the finds were also continued.

2018

The year 2018 was the final season of excavations on Divriği Castle. The season started with the surface cleaning. The studies carried out in recent years concentrated on the Cave region in the Inner Wall area. In the works carried out here, the rubble and soil layers that have accumulated over time on the rock are removed. As a result of these studies, rock floor and remains of the wall structure were unearthed on one side.

As the work on the upper level progressed, three spaces belonging to a building began to reveal (Photo 20).

Photo 20- Anonymous Structure, General View from the Southwest

The opening part of the building, which will be defined as anonymous for now, measures approximately 5.45x12.15 m. As far as can be seen, it consists of three rectangular units' side by side. When the part that remains under the ground opens, it will be possible to make the evaluation of its plan and possible function more realistically. Due to the data obtained from the area and the fact that the unit in the middle is arranged differently than the others, it is possible that it may be an iwan. The measurements of the visible part of the unit are clockwise from the north on 3.00, 3.30, 3.80 and 2.90 m in size. It is seen that the floor of the space, which reflects a trapezoidal plan, is arranged higher than the side units (Photo 21).

Photo 21- Anonymous Structure, Aerial View

This is one of the main reasons why we consider it as an iwan. The second possibility is the presence of 3 stones in the middle of the space that served as carriers for the wooden supports. The aforementioned stones are placed approximately in the middle of the space and at 0.55 and 0.70 m intervals from each other. Around them is a compressed soil which suggests the floor existed on that ground. After it is fully opened, it will be possible to fully understand the function of the building to which the spaces belong. Small finds from the area, most of which have moved to this section, are of no help in this regard.

The building, which has begun to open, has an important contribution to the architectural texture of the area. The space extending in the north-south direction indicates the existence of other structures in this direction and level. With the work to be done in the next seasons, there is a strong possibility to reach more spaces and structures on this level.

4 FIELD INTRODUCTION (Photo 22)

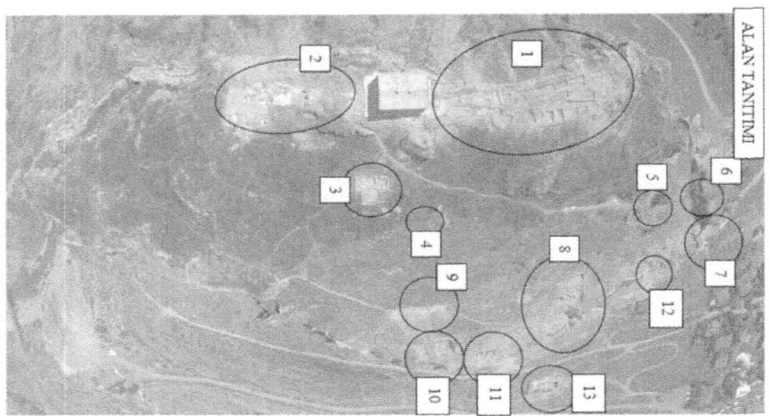

Photo 22- Excavation Areas, General View

1 - Flag Area

The area we call the Flag Area because of the Flagpole measures approximately 25 x 80 m (Photo 23).

Photo 23- Flag Area, looking at North

A large part of it has been unearthed with the excavations carried out from the 2011 season to the present time. There are still piles of soil in the west and east that need to be removed.[30] It was observed that the spaces revealed by the excavation of the area were shaped in accordance with the topography of the area. It can be understood that there is a narrow street and a wide inner courtyard between the two series of spaces that use each other's walls in common in the West and East. One of the units exposed in the south of the courtyard has a quality stone floor covering (Photo 24).

Photo 24- Flag Area, After Excavation, Ground Detail

---

[30] The average age of the Divriği Castle Excavation team does not even reach 20 from time to time. It has not been found suitable for now to work especially in the east of the area without taking the necessary precautions.

It is possible to date floor covering in this state to the 13th century at the latest. The walls on the aforementioned floor are considered as late period annexes due to both material-technical aspects and their geometrical relations with the ground.[31] In addition to the walls made with the dry wall technique without binder material, partially Khorasan mortared walls and a small section of mudbrick wall material were found in the area.

It is understood from the ruins that the places in this section were surrounded by a destroyed city wall in the east. A similar situation is true for the western part. There are also remains of a strong wall in the west. Perhaps that is why there is talk of an Ahmedek.[32] Considering its proximity to the Castle Mosque, which is the most important structure of the Inner Castle, it can be argued that the spaces are more suitable for the harem.

The large rectangular space located in the south of the inner courtyard looks like a ward built in the late period with its crenellated windows on the west wall. The geometry of the walls built in the dry wall technique is also slightly different in terms of the topographic structure of the area.

---

[31] The walls and tandoors on the ground were added in a later period.

[32] Ahmedek is a sheltered area used as a dungeon from time to time, and where the Sultan and his family took refuge in times of war. The best-known example in Anatolia is in Konya. However, the most important feature of Ahmedek is that it is built in a section where you can easily get away from the area if there is a serious danger at the time of war. In this state, it is not possible to talk about an Ahmedek in Divriği.

The artifacts uncovered scattered in this section showed that there was at least a monumental burial structure or place in the area. Extremely damaged tile and stucco pieces are traces of important structures in the castle (Photo 25).[33]

Photo 25- Flag Area, Tile Plate

However, the fact that the finds are not in their original places indicates that they were brought by transport.

---

[33] Divriği Castle is a settlement that has been destroyed with its entire area from top to bottom. There are different accounts about the exit date of the last houses from the castle, but it is certain that it has never been the same after the 17th century. This is thought-provoking for a settlement that has not seen serious warfare.

2 - Cistern Area (Photo 26)

Photo 26- Cistern Area, Looking at South

This section was named the Cistern Area because of the 5.30x8.00 m sized barrel-vaulted cistern located approximately 40 m north of the Castle Mosque. Geophysical surveys made from time to time show that other cisterns may be found around the existing cistern.[34]

In addition, as stated before, it was decided to clean the surrounding of the Castle Mosque in order to protect it from possible fires, and work was carried out in a band of approximately 60 meters in this area.

During the studies, wall remains belonging to five rectangular shaped rooms of different sizes and many cisterns/storages carved into the rock were unearthed. There is no data yet on the existence of a cistern of the expected size and depth. However, the details seen on the rock floor [deep storage pits, canals that seem to have been made for water

---

[34] Therefore, the area poses a danger to visitors. Since the warning signs were removed by unknown persons, it was decided to excavate them and check them.

collection, blood pits] were evaluated as traces showing that the site was originally used for ceremonial purposes (Photo 27). The top of the wells was covered with an iron grid to prevent damage to the visitors.

Photo 27- Cistern Area, After Excavation, General View

3 - 2009 Trench-Manufacturing Workshop

The evaluations made as a result of the geophysical surveys carried out in the area in 2007 showed that a group of spaces may have been used with different functions, approximately 30 m west of the Castle Mosque. For this reason, in the 2009 working season, studies were started in an area of approximately 9.00x12.00 m to provide some geophysical survey studies in the aforementioned region.[35]

The data from the opened section showed that the geophysical method is healthy. Five adjacent spaces were unearthed, two on the west and three on the east (Photo 28).

Photo 28- 2009 Trench, Workshop

---

[35] The method called archeogeophysics has been used by almost all archaeological excavations in our country in recent years. The success rate in Divriği Castle is very low because the mining area of the region affects sensitive instruments adversely. This method did not work for most of the area, so what we call the 2009 trench is important. The results obtained have been published.

Two of the rooms in the east have five oven (Tandır) of different shapes and depths.[36] It is certain that the places point to a workshop whose type we do not know today (Photo 29).

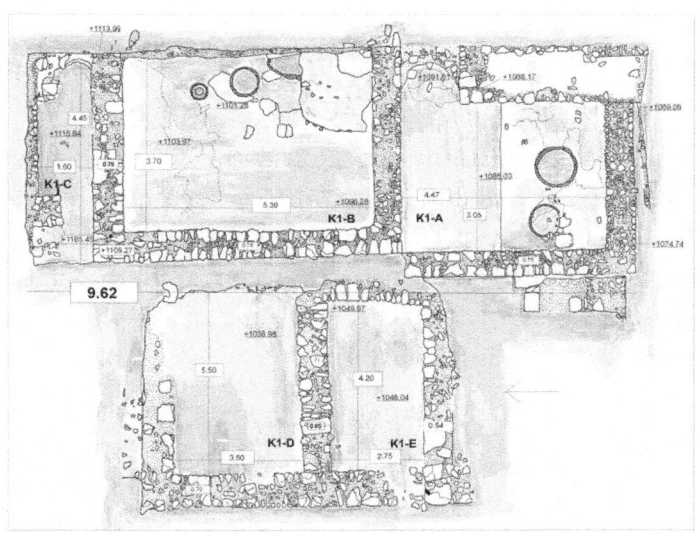

Photo 29- 2009 Trench, Workshop, Plan

---

[36] The number of oven increased to six with the stove, which was understood to have been placed inside the wall during the consolidation works carried out later on.

Another striking detail regarding this section is the female skeleton unearthed in the 1.60x4.45 m corridor section in the north. For an unknown reason, it was understood that she died by staying under the wall that collapsed on her.[37]

4 - Inner Wall

Although the situation between the bastions was partially clarified during the work carried out to determine the entrance to the inner-city wall, detailed information about the gate could not be obtained. It is seen that the wall between the bastions was overhauled, and some changes were made in different periods (Photo 30).

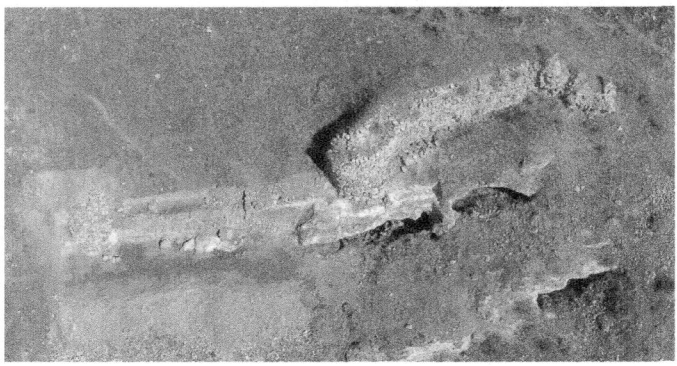

Photo 30- Inner Wall, After Excavation, General View

---

[37] The faculty members of Cumhuriyet University, Faculty of Letters, Department of Anthropology are working on the old woman from Divriği who died due to a collapsed wall.

It was seen that spaces were created with walls extending in the east- west direction, which were added to the west of the city wall, adjacent to it. The study needs to be developed further south for a more precise assessment.[38]

5 – Staircase (Photo 31)

Photo 31- Staircase, General View from the East

Most of the road used by visitors consists of sloping rocky ground. In order for visitors of all ages to climb this difficult path safely, a staircase that can stand on its own weight

---

[38] The most suitable place for the inner wall gate is here and between the two bastions located further south. Final judgment on this issue will be given after the excavation of the southern section.

without damaging the ground has been designed and implemented on site.[39]

6 - Vaulted Spaces

In the southern part of the outer wall of Divriği Castle, there are two vaulted units built for the use of guards.[40] The aforementioned places were cleaned before the repair works (Photo 32).

Photo 32- Vaulted Units, After Cleaning

---

[39] Even watching the staircase from afar, that uses the conditions of the ground on which it is applied, gives great pleasure. Thankful to those who contributed.

[40] It is also said that they were palace places, but this is not possible due to their location in the castle. They were built to control the south, and they have narrow crenellated windows suitable for this.

The fillings on the floors and intermediate walls have been cleaned. The finds from the places showed that they were used for a long time. Perhaps they should be among the last abandoned places in the field (Photo 33).

Photo 33- Vaulted Units, Restoration Work

7 - Sultan's Gate

Photo 34- Sultan's Gate, Aerial View

The gate, located in the southwest corner of the walls (Photo 34), is called by this name due to its proximity to the Divriği

Great Mosque and its possible connection with a road. It is not known how the exit was made to the gate, which was filled and closed at an unknown date.[41]

Photo 35- Sultan's Gate, Upper Section, View to the North

---

[41] It is not clear when the gate, which was covered with Khorasan mortar, rubble stone and cut stone material in places, took this appearance. Two important times are under evaluation in this regard. The first is the arrival of the Mongols to Divriği in 1277. The Mongolian commander, who did not like the way he was greeted, ordered the demolition of the walls. It is not known how much damage was done to the walls, but it is possible that the gate was symbolically destroyed. The second event is the Celali Revolts that shook the Ottoman Empire in the 17th century. There are records that the castle was captured by groups that attempted to revolt during this period. The possibility of the gate being damaged during these riots is also evaluated. The only thing that is certain is that the rubble filling heaped behind the gate was carried out in two different stages. In both, the level of living can be clearly understood due to the remains of the hearth and oven.

At the start of the 2010 excavation season, several of the top row stones of the bastion north of the gate were visible on the surface (Photo 35).

The works started in a trench measuring 10.00x10.00 m in the area have been improved over the years and our knowledge about the gate has increased thanks to this.

One of the most important details revealed by the studies is the traces showing that the gate has at least two phases. It is understood that the first gate was located in the east-west direction facing the Divriği Great Mosque (Photo 36).

Photo 36- Sultan's Gate, After Excavation, Aerial View

Later, a long wall piece with a lion relief was built in front of the gate and it was hidden from view.[42]

Immediately after the entrance, the presence of a pointed arched niche on the south wall was revealed. The niche, whose floor is higher than the entrance floor, was probably made for a guard to stand. Behind the gate and the entrance to the east, there is a corridor in the north-south direction. It is a feature seen in military structures such as castles or city gates that people move forward by changing direction. No inscription data has yet been found in the area opened in the interior.[43]

To the north of the corridor, there is a low-arched inner gate in the north-south direction. Later studies revealed that there was a 4.00x4.00 m space behind the gate. Since the entire rubble fill in the space has not been removed yet, it has not yet been understood how the transition to the castle area was made. However, it is estimated that it turns towards the east again. It was observed that there was an oven on the ground reaching towards the west of the area.[44]

---

[42] It is not possible to know exactly when this change took place, but for now it is possible to think that it was between the days when the construction was started and the years 1236-1252 during the construction of the bastion known as Arslanburç (Lion Bastion). The subject is still being followed.

[43] The eastern wall of the corridor is not yet fully opened. It is highly probable that an inscription will be encountered after the 3.00 m thick layer of rubble is removed.

[44] Since it does not have a chimney, it looks more like a shallow hearth.

It is a great loss that its cover has not survived to the present day. There are no ornamental elements on the walls built with cut-stone material and with Khorasan mortar.[45]

It is among the obtained data that the walls of the spaces exposed at the upper level were built on this infrastructure.[46] The second phase walls at the top have a neat scheme in themselves, and at least one of the units must definitely be the kitchen due to the stove data. It is not possible to say anything definite about the functions of the other units, but it is certain that it is a **residence**.

---

[45] On one of the jambs carrying the arch, there is a small niche that is not too deep. If it is not related to the locking mechanism of the door, it must have been used for a lighting device such as an oil lamp.

[46] Perhaps the relationship between the two phases can also lead to an idea about the filling time of the gate and its surroundings. If they deliberately used the walls below as a foundation while the upper spaces were built, they must be the ones who filled it. It is possible to reach more data on this subject in the later stages of the excavation.

8 - Main Gate

As mentioned earlier, work on the Main Gate started in 2010 (Photo 37).

Photo 37- Main Gate, Before Excavation, General View

Unlike the Sultan's Gate in the south, the Main Gate was used for passage to the castle. Before the removal of the rubble, which was almost filled up to the surviving arch of the gate, it was aimed to relieve the stress in the back and the work was started (Photo 38).

Photo 38- Main Gate, After Excavation, General View

Terracing has been done in this section because the land is rising especially in the southern part of the gate (Photo 39).[47]

Photo 39- Main Gate, Ana Kapı, Terracing, General View

One of the first results reached during the studies is the presence of a rectangular building in the north just behind the gate (Photo 40).

---

[47] An important detail regarding the excavation is that the rubble in the area is heavily calcareous since it belongs to mudbrick structures that were later demolished for various reasons. After a winter has passed, there is no flow or loss in the profiles due to the lime it contains. The situation has been monitored by us for years and there is no change. Unfortunately, humans are responsible for the destruction, not nature.

Photo 40- North of the Main Gate, Masjid, General View

It was observed that the building, which was built with rubble stone material, had a compacted soil floor. Although its cover has been destroyed, there is no doubt that it was made with an old technique used in Divriği until the last century. The mentioned technique is adobe walls and wooden cover on a rubble stone foundation. Remains of wooden pillars adjacent to the walls belonging to the supports carrying the cover were found. Another data regarding the space is that its walls are plastered with stucco. Due to its location, it was considered to be a control function at first glance and was called a police station. However, as the work progressed, and the building was studied more carefully, it was understood that it was a masjid.

It is certain that the Castle Mosque, the only surviving structure in the castle, is not open to general use due to its location. It is normal to have a worship building in the area, especially below. After this feature was understood, the unknown building was named Lower Castle Masjid. Due to its location and material-technical features, it dates to the 15th century as the earliest.

It is not possible to remove all the rubble accumulated over the years behind the gate immediately.[48] However, the removal of the accumulated rubble in the gate corridor continues. These studies showed that the cover of the gate corridor and the floor were destroyed. In this section, after the damage caused by an unknown reason, second or third phase construction was carried out on the corridor walls. On the east side of the south wall of the entrance corridor, on the corner where we consider that the road turns towards the north is a shallow niche for the guards. The presence of a niche with a pointed arch is important as it shows that the road after the gate continues upwards.[49]

---

[48] The wall to the south of the gate is not in good condition since its cladding was also opened, and the expansion of the terraces to the south was postponed in order not to cause much movement in this section.

[49] After this part of the wall is repaired, the removal of the rubble will continue.

After these works were carried out in the northern and southern sections, along with the corridor, terracing was also made on the eastern slope of the gate in order to prevent the flow that may occur due to the deepening of the gate area (Photo 41).

Photo 41- East of the Main Gate, Terracing

Some interesting results were obtained with this study. First of all, a space with cut-stone pavement and Khorasan mortar, which started to be exposed, helped to understand the depth of the ground inside the castle behind the gate with the stone paved road data right in front of it.[50]

---

[50] The most important problem of the area is the thick rubble layer that has flowed from above and accumulated behind the wall. With the study done here, it was seen that the ground is not at the same depth everywhere. The

At the lowest part of the aforementioned terracing work, a private bath began to emerge, which was later closed and understood to have undergone changes (Photo 42).

Photo 42- East of the Main Gate, Residence with Bath

Along with the bath, walls belonging to some spaces were revealed on the terrace, and it was understood that the houses in the castle were built on top of each other in this section. However, the material of the walls other than the bathhouse is rubble stone and it is seen that they were built without the use of binding material.

---

rock floor on which the wall was built rises from west to east and its depth is not the same everywhere. Rock ground very close to the surface can be encountered. It was observed that the walls of the Anonymous building, which is the deepest section in the area, were also built on the rock floor. The elevation, which is approximately -5,00 meters in the anonymous structure, decreases to around -1.00 meters as you go south and then deepens again.

The construction above a certain level must have been carried out in the late period, as in the other parts of the castle.

9 - Rock Tomb Area

There are two burial chambers opened on the rock slope approximately 100 m north of the main gate (Photo 43). It is still possible to see many rock structure details on the approximately 250 x 400-meter rock promontory on which the Divriği Castle is built. Other than the burial chambers, these details include niches, cisterns, storage pits, blood pits, tombs with destroyed covers, mortars carved into the rock, water channels, and even rock places with some collapsed walls.

Photo 43- Rock Tomb Area, Aerial View

Undoubtedly, the rock structure details are from the days of the Iron Age in the region. The shaping of the rocks, which are very hard in places, could only be possible with tools made of iron, which is a hard metal. In general, in Anatolia, the Iron Age, BC. 1 is thought to have started to live with a thousand people. Undoubtedly, Divriği and its surroundings must have played a leading role in this regard due to its rich mineral deposits.[51]

It is known that the most important Iron Age culture in this part of Anatolia was the Urartian. It is possible that the details of the rock architecture can be dated to this period at the latest. However, we do not have any other data to prove the existence of Urartu apart from the rock spaces. A piece that was found during the rock-cut tomb site excavations in 2014 was dated to the Urartian period for the same reason, and thus, the Urartian presence could be sampled with a find for the first time (Photo 44). It is possible that more different works will emerge as the studies progress.

---

[51] Although there is no exact data, the importance of the region and even Divriği, perhaps in terms of mining, dates to the 1st century BC. There is a possibility that it took place even before a thousand. For an important study on the subject, see K. R. Maxwell-Hyslop, "A Preliminary Survey of the Historical and Geographical Evidence", *Iraq*, Vol. 36, No. 1/2, 1974, pp. 139-154.

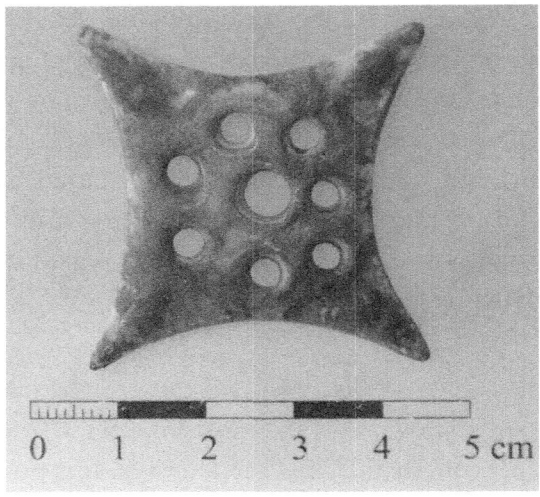

Photo 44- Find from the Urartian Period

Two more burial chambers were found during the southward opening of the rock tomb area in 2014 and 2015 (Photo 45). The rock details unearthed together with the burial chambers show that it was a cult area in its original state.[52] The fact that such ceremonial formations are encountered in different areas shows that the area on which a castle was built in the Middle Ages was an important cult center for its immediate surroundings.

---

[52] The large niches on the rock surface to the south of the two new burial chambers unearthed in the area suggest that there have been attempts to increase the number of rooms, but this was abandoned for some reason and large niches were opened.

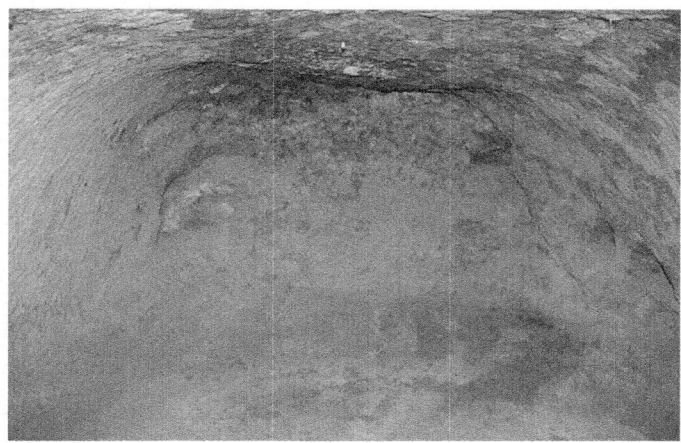

Photo 45- Rock Tomb Chamber, Interior View

The fact that the data on the subject is developing in this direction indicates that the first settlement of Divriği might have been in a place other than the area where the castle was built. It is understood that the construction of a large animal relief was started on the mentioned rock surface, but it was left unfinished as in the other sections.[53]

---

[53] The relief, whose head part unfortunately has not survived, must belong to a bull as far as it can be understood from the traces and body structure. The existence of the relief, which is currently only visible to us, will most likely be supported by other examples that may come to light. The field is suitable for such applications.

Work in 2015 continued in the upper part of the same area. As the rock surfaces are opened, the castle will have a much more impressive silhouette due to the details on them. During the work carried out in the upper section, many details carved on the rock were encountered. Although there is no mound in the area, the view of the rock floor is getting more impressive day by day.

With niches carved into the rock, hearths, pools, oven placed on the ground and walls added to create space, the change of the settlement that lasted for thousands of years can be easily observed. Although it is thought that the area is considered to be a residential area in its final form, the presence of pools of different depths and plastered walls are details that show that we are dealing with a kind of workshop. It will be possible to evaluate the subject more accurately with future data.

10 - Anonymous Structure

The building, located approximately 80 m north of the Main Gate, was named Anonymous within the scope of the study, since its function has not been understood yet (Photo 46). The square-shaped structure has a side size of 10 m and was built with rubble stone. There are traces of stucco in the southwestern corner of the building, in which Khorasan mortar was used as the binding material, near the ground level. It was observed that the ground reached in the same section was not flat and the rock floor was not level.

Photo 46- Anonymous Building, Before Excavation, General View

It is understood that the place was covered with a dome, due to the remains of the corner triangle that can still be seen on the wall corners and on the upper level. However, it is not yet certain whether this belongs to a single dome.[54] There is a spiral body pile made of brick material on the ground. Since the ruined item has not been opened sufficiently yet, its function could not be understood (Photo 47).

---

[54] As in some similar examples, it is thought that the space may have been divided into four units by arches thrown on a support in the center. The subject of four units covered with a 5 m diameter dome is being evaluated.

Photo 47- Anonymous Building, After Excavation, General View

The entrance of the place, that has no sign of entrance on the east and west walls, must be from the east or north. The situation will be better understood as studies advance.

11 - 3rd Bastion Area (Photo 48)

Photo 48- 3rd Bastion Area, Before Excavation

Following a wall noticed on the ground during the cleaning of the area, the second advanced building in terms of material and technique was encountered. The related building was evaluated as a small part of a residence with a private bath. As it was mentioned in the Main Gate section, there are residences with private baths and possibly underfloor heating in Divriği Castle. Along with a small temperature section, the water reservoir and the furnace section to the west were partially opened (Photo 49).

Photo 49- 3rd Bastion Area, After Excavation

The walls of the small bath unit, which had its share of destruction in the area, were built with bricks and plastered. There are decorations made with red paint in places on the stucco.[55] It is still early to date the site. It is not clear whether the place in front of us is a Mengüjek or Mamluk structure. With the opening of the adjacent spaces, the subject will be clarified.

12 - South of the Main Gate, Front of the Wall

In the west, most of the walls have been destroyed. The rubble flowing out from the collapsed sections is piled up right in front of the wall and must be removed. The subject is being developed in parallel with the roadwork that will provide the connection between the Castle and the Ulu Mosque. In order to facilitate the repair works to be carried out in this section, the rubble at the bottom of the city wall has been started to be removed. It was seen that a space of 2.50x8.50 m was built between the two bastions that were destroyed during the works.

The interesting detail about the place is that the floor is stone paved and the bastions on both the north and south are ruined. No trace of the entrance has been found yet, but it can be easily understood from the additional trace seen in the material that the place was added later.

---

[55] Paintings are cleaned every year and covered with chemicals for protection.

13 - Upper Church

The pile of rubble accumulated in the building was cleared by working for three seasons between 2007 and 2009 (Photo 50).[56] The building, whose name has not been clarified yet, draws attention with its dimensions and material-technical features.[57]

Photo 50- Upper Church, After Excavation, General View

---

[56] In the building, which is almost inside the city, illegal excavations were carried out by unknown people after the excavation team. Despite the efforts of the relevant units, the building is a frequented place for diners and unfortunately our efforts to illuminate the area were in vain.

[57] It is also seen that metal tensioners were used in the structure, which was built with smooth cut stone material. Among the church building materials, cut stones belonging to the castle are concentrated.

It is understood from the traces left on a very small part of the walls that the interior was decorated with stucco. It is noteworthy that its apse faces north, but the subject of orientation in the late period is not subject to strict rules as in the medieval practices.[58]

On August 17, 2009, a column body, possibly engraved with the date of the church's construction [1268 H./ M.1852] was unearthed (Photo 51). In the same season, the opening under the main apse was emptied. Among the other finds in this area are two coins, pieces of icons [made with plaster coating on wood and gilding on blue], writing fragments that are thought to be Torah pages, as well as pieces of stucco and molded architectural elements.

---

[58] The fact that the apses were in the north was the most difficult one among the subjects of analysis and evaluation. It is seen in a few applications in Anatolia [in one or two rock churches in the Cappadocia valley], but it seems that there are more examples in Europe. Since the building is an Armenian church, the influence of Yerevan was emphasized in the orientation, but Yerevan is located in the northeast of Divriği. The fact that it is a late period structure and the presence of the Armenian community in the Kalealtı district, and the topographical conditions of the available area, must have also affected the position of the apses. Similarly, the apses of the Lower Church are in the north.

Photo 51- Upper Church, Column Body, 1268/1851-52

5 FINDS

During the studies carried out between 2007 and 2015, a total of 3576 pieces were recorded in the excavation inventory. The number of quality finds is increasing every year.[59]

When the finds are analyzed numerically, 1278 glass bracelets[60], 1150 stone balls[61], 226 coins[62], 215 pipes, 257 beads and 104 stuccos draw attention as the most important finds.[63]

Small Finds

Small finds unearthed during the Divriği Castle excavation can be examined in four groups as ceramic, metal, glass and bone. Small finds, the richest group of which is ceramics, can be evaluated with the analogy method and the historical process of Divriği, as they were found in a mixed form. Although there are very few, pottery fragments belonging to the Late Roman and even older periods, the Urartian, shed light on the history of the castle. It is noteworthy

---

[59] In addition to those unearthed by excavation, all-natural iron ore samples found in the area are collected to be exhibited as evidence of iron working.
[60] Bracelets made of glass material are mostly recovered as fragments. There are very few complete pieces. The fact that the number is increasing every year is important because it shows that glass works are produced in Divriği.
[61] Stone cannonballs, which are generally found in the lower part, are used for the defense of the castle. They are made of different sizes and types of stones. They are kept for display.
[62] Few of the coins are legible. No Mengüjek coin has been found yet.
[63] A small part of the samples recovered can be exhibited in the Museum.

that the examples in the finds are concentrated in the 12th and 14th century.

Among the <u>ceramic finds</u>; A small number of rims, body and base fragments belonging to red slip ware dishes and bowls and the bottom of an *unguentarium* (Photo 52) of the castle settlement of the Late Roman-Early Byzantine Period [4th -6th century].

Photo 52- Unguentarium

In unglazed ceramic vessel types; jugs, amphorae, small jar, pithos [large jar] and rims, bases, bodies, strainers, spouts and handles of cooking/storage vessels, rims, and bases of bowls as well as small bowls and oil lamp fragments that give full form, and spherical conical vessels. Tripods draw attention as parts and furnace material.

Jug and amphorae are generally reddish yellow, with additives, produced from high quality dough. Flat or round-section handles on these vessels with flat or everted rims, spherical body and flat base join the shoulder starting from the rim or neck (Photo 53-54).

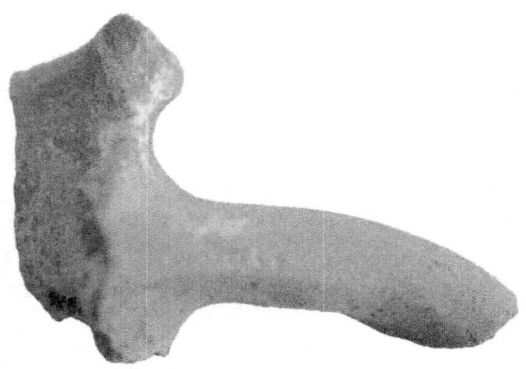

Photo 53- Unglazed Jug Handle Mouthpiece

Photo 54- Unglazed Handles

It is understood from the fragments that there are strainer and spout types of the jugs (Photo 55-56).

Photo 55- Unglazed Fragment of Jug with Strainer

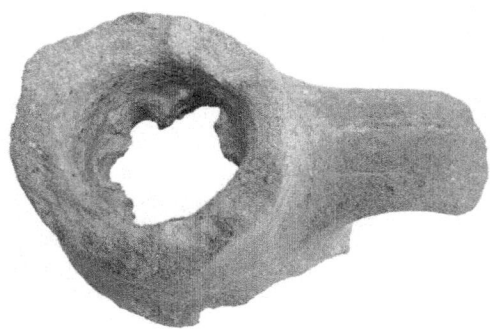

Photo 56- Unglazed Fragment of Jug with Strainer

It is possible to examine the containers used for storage in two groups as small jars and pithos. Small jars contain additives and red clay. Two main groups were observed in the clays as coarse and high quality. The forms are examples with a spherical body and a flat base that generally narrow at the mouth (Photo 57).

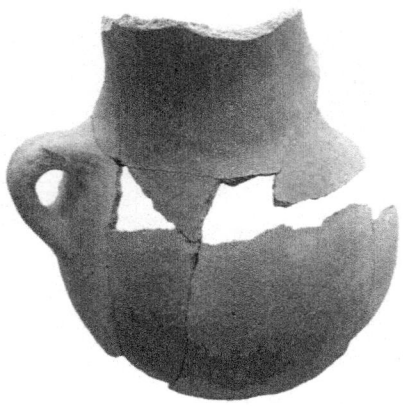

Photo 57- Unglazed Jug

Thin and thick-walled body parts show that the wall changes according to the material stored inside (Photo 58-60).

Photo 58- Unglazed Jug Mouthpiece

Photo 59- Unglazed Jug Mouthpiece

Photo 60- Unglazed Jug Mouthpiece

As for decoration on jars; grooves surrounding the body, regular or irregular zigzag motifs made with thick-tipped tools, successive circular and oval shaped concave cavities made by finger pressing are seen (Photo 61-63).

Photo 61- Unglazed Fragment of Decorated Body

Photo 62- Unglazed Fragment of Decorated Body

Photo 63- Unglazed Fragment of Decorated Body

Broken mouth fragments have survived from the pithos. In thick-walled examples with thick and everted rims, the everted rim is generally flat, while in some examples, finger-press decoration surrounds the rim (Photo 64).

Photo 64- Unglazed Pithos Mouthpiece

Small bowls are among the vessels that were used intensively during the settlement (Photo 65). The fact that the inner surfaces of the samples were burned suggests that they may have been used for illumination.

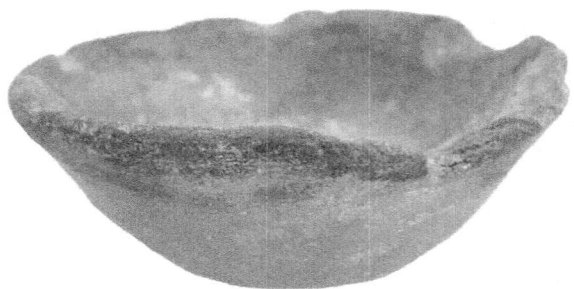

Photo 65- Unglazed Small Bowl / Lamp

In glazed ceramics, the rim, body and pedestals of plates and bowls, as well as oil lamp fragments provide rich examples of decoration techniques and motifs, and give information about daily life, production and trade in the castle. In glazed ceramics, multi-colored vessels made with a single color glazed and painted sgraffito technique attract attention. Parallel lines on the rims and bodies, and floral motifs are common in multicolored glazed ceramics. This group displays similarities with ceramics dating to the 13th century, which were mainly found in the Mediterranean region such as Antakya, Al-Mina, St. Symeon Harbor, Anamur, Cyprus and eastern Anatolia settlements (Photo 66).

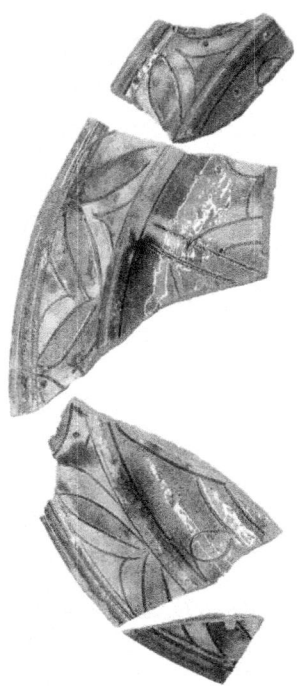

Photo 66- Glazed Ceramic Dish Fragments

Although St. Symeon Harbor is generally accepted as the place of production, the discovery of this group in different regions indicates that it is an integral part of all Eastern Mediterranean societies [Christian, Islamic] and trade, according to S. Redford.[64]

Examples decorated with sgraffito and champlevé techniques also occupy an important place in medieval glazed ceramics. Human and animal figures[65], plant [leaf, palmette, flower] motifs and knitting motifs draw attention to the rim, pedestal and body fragments of plates, pots and bowls. Colors [shades of green and yellow] used in technical and single or multi-colored glazes show similarities with the 12th -13th century Byzantine, Seljuk and Principalities period ceramics (Photo 67-69).

---

[64] S. Redford, " 'Port Saint Symeon Seramiği' Denilen Hatay ve Çukurova Bölgesi Sgraffito Seramiği", *V. Ortaçağ ve Türk Dönemi Kazı ve Araştırmaları Sempozyumu. 19-20 April 2001. Bildiriler.* Ankara 2001, pp. 485-490.

[65] M. Acara Eser, "Divriği Kale Kazısı Sırlı Seramiklerinden Kuş ve Balık Figürlü Örnekler/Glazed Pottery Examples With Bird and Fish Figured From Divriği Castle Excavations", *SDÜ Fen-Edebiyat FakültesiSosyal Bilimler Dergisi,* 48, 2019, pp. 41-60.

Photo 67- Glazed Ceramic Fragment with Human Figure

Photo 68- Glazed Ceramic Fragment with Fish Figure

Photo 69- Glazed Ceramic Fragments with Knitted Motifs

The most important data in terms of ceramics are semi-finished samples. Glazed samples with the same motifs as the semi-finished ceramics with geometric, plant or fish figures suggest the existence of ceramic production in Divriği (Photo 70-72). [66]

Photo 70- Semi-finished Ceramic Fragment with Fish Figure

---

[66] M. Acara Eser, "Divriği Kale Kazısı Sırlı Seramik Buluntuları: İlk Sonuçlar ve Yerel Üretim İzleri/Glazed Pottery From Divriği Castle Excavations: First Results and Local Production Traces", *Hacettepe Üniversitesi Edebiyat Fakültesi Dergisi*, 37 (1), 2020, pp. 136-153.

Photo 71- Semi-finished Ceramic Fragments

Photo 72- Glazed Ceramic Bowl

In addition to ceramic fragments similar to turquoise glazed vessels known to have been produced in Iran in the 12th century and dated to the Anatolian Seljuks in the 13th century, there are also pedestals and body fragments of jugs belonging to the Late Ottoman period, completely covered with green glaze inside and outside were found in the area. A piece of multicolored pottery from the 16th century in which white clay and red color was used. Also, pieces of European porcelain belonging to the 19th-20th century were found.

Among the ceramics belonging to the Ottoman period, there are fragments belonging to blue-white Kütahya cups and Iznik ceramics called Milet work, dating back to the 14th and 15th century. The base, mouth and body of the jug with a green glaze inside and outside of the late 19th and early 20th century, and pieces of porcelain are among the finds pointing to the life of the Castle dating back to the 20th century.

As a result, it can be said that the finds belonging to the Roman and Byzantine Periods are few. On the other hand, examples from the Zeuxippus family dated to the 11th and 13th century and potsherds decorated with sgraffito and champlevé techniques are indicators of commercial relations with the Byzantium in the castle under Mengüjeks (Photo 73). In glazed ceramics, examples produced in the 12th-13th century are abundant, as well as ceramics from the Late Ottoman period and porcelain pieces, although in small numbers. These data show that the castle was a residential area from the 12th century to the beginning of the 20th century.

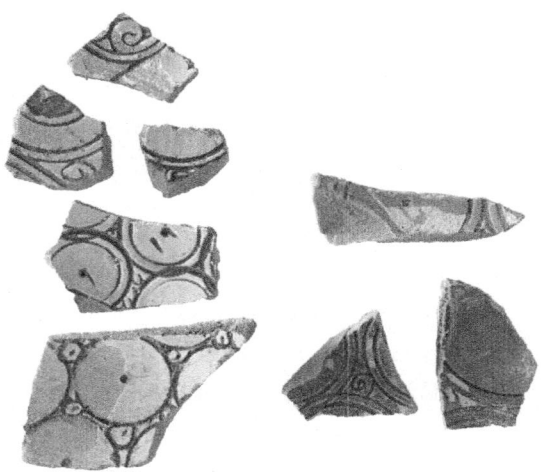

Photo 73- Glazed Ceramic Fragments belonging to the Zeuxippus Family

Metal objects; One of the earliest finds among the metal objects is the small bronze cross arm dating back to the 6th-7th century, with the ends of the arms ending in two circles and decorated with concentric circle motifs (Photo 74).

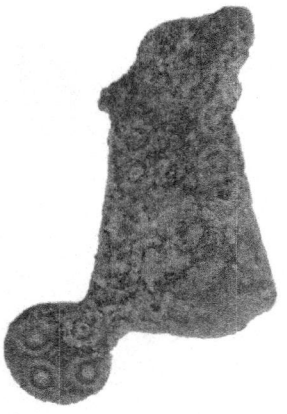

Photo 74- Bronze Arm of the Cross

Copper rings from the Early and Middle Byzantine Periods decorated with concentric circle motifs, a lead seal probably from the 11th century, a bronze arrow ring decorated with floral motifs from the Ottoman Period, the polyhedral bronze dirham with similar examples from the 12th-13th century in the Seljuk Period and 15th-16th century in the Ottoman Period, the bronze dirham with an open middle, from the Ottoman Period, whose tughra cannot be deciphered, but with similar examples seen in the 18th century (Photo 75),

Photo 75- Bronze Dirham

belt buckles belonging to the Byzantine and Ottoman periods can be counted among the important metal finds (Photo 76-77).[67]

---

[67] For the similarity of the polyhedral dirham seen in the Seljuk and Ottoman periods, see. G. Kurkman, *Anatolian Weights and Measures*. Istanbul 2003, p. 226, no. 95, p. 232, no. 119, p. 235, no. 131; For the similarity of the circular dirham, see. ibid, p. 248, no. 180.

Photo 76- Copper Alloy Belt Buckle

Photo 77- Copper Alloy Belt Buckle

The 17th century Dutch coin, on the other hand, draws attention as a memento of a traveler or merchant who had been to the Castle during the Ottoman period (Photo 78).[68]

Photo 78- Silver, Dutch Coin

---

[68] M. Acara Eser, " Divriği Kale Kazısında Bulunan Bir "Leeuwendaalder (Aslanlı Dolar)"in İzinde/On The Trail A "Leeuwendaalder (Lion-dollar)" Found in Divriği Castle Excavation", *Turkish Studies,* 16 (7), 2021, pp. 1-8.

Glass finds; the light blue bottle mouth and body parts found in the "Cistern", a light green ring and two small light green handles found in the "Cave" and a light green colored, hollow folded rim, a concave base and body in the "Main Gate". Except for the body fragments, all the finds were found at the "Sultan's Gate". Among the examples are mouth-neck, pedestal and body fragments of various sized bottles, flat rims and hollow folded rimmed pedestals of glass and goblet-type containers (Photo 79-80),

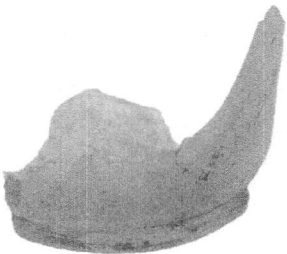

Photo 79- Glass Base

Photo 80- Glass Base

a transparent, hollow-folded rimmed round window glass piece (Photo 81),

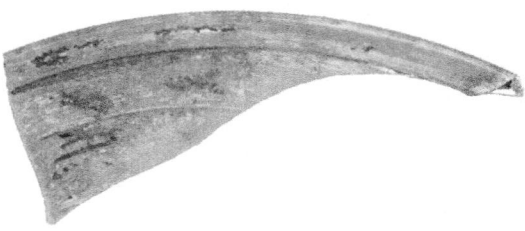

Photo 81- Fragment of Window Glass

and pieces of lighting tools such as hollow oil lamp sticks, and pieces of transparent, sliced, blue-colored glass fiber decorated vessels (Photo 82).

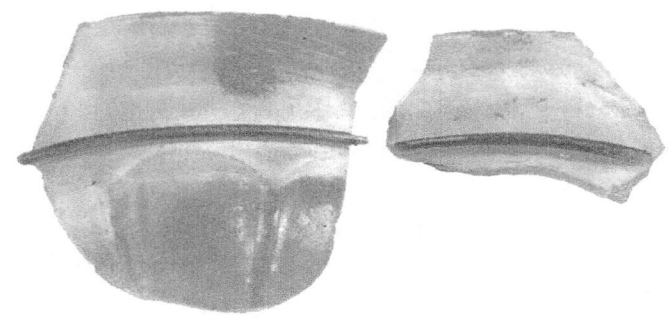

Photo 82- Glass Vessel Fragments

Among the glasses whose similar examples were found in the excavations of Corinth[69], Sardis[70], Demre[71] and Kubad

---

[69] G. R. Davidson, *Corinth. Vol.12: The Minor Objects*. Princeton 1952, see p. 108, fig.12 [for rim and folded pedestals]; p. 118, fig. 17 [for concave plinths]; p. 113, fig. 14 [for mouths].

[70] A. von Harden, *Ancient and Byzantine Glass from Sardis*. Harvard 1980, see Pl. 23 [for lamp with hollow rod]; pl. 24-25 [for pedestals]; pl. 26 [for mouths].

[71] Ö. Çömezoğlu, *Demre Aziz Nikolaos Kilisesi Kazılarında 1996-1999 Yılları Arasında Bulunan Aydınlatma İşlevli Cam Eserler*. Hacettepe Üniversitesi Yayımlanmamış Yüksek Lisans Tezi, Ankara 2001, see Lev. IV/5-7, Lev. V/13 [for lamp with hollow rod]; Lev. VIII/38-41 [for concave plinths]; Lev. XV [for mouths]; Lev. XXV/137, 141, 144-145 [for hollow plinths], Lev. XXX-XXXI [for folded edge window glass].

Abad Palace[72] in Anatolia, the closest similar pieces of glass and goblets were found among the finds of Kubad Abad Palace dating back to the 12th-13th century.

Among the glass finds, bracelet fragments with various colors and decorations hold an important place (Photo 83). The main color is black, dark navy blue, and blue is intense, but there are also yellow and white bracelet pieces. In the decorations, apart from the spiral groove of the body, decorations created by dripping glass paste of different colors – especially white - on the body at equal intervals, spirals formed by wrapping glass fibers of different colors [white, yellow, blue, dark blue] on the body, and wave motif-like decorations made with different colors on the body are seen. Pieces similar to a blue glass bracelet fragment dated to the 6th-7th century in Rusafa, to the 10th-14th century in Sardes, to the 11th century in Saraçhane, and to the 8th-12th century in the excavations of the Church of St. Nicholas in Demre shows the continuity of glass bracelets throughout cultures.[73]

---

[72] Z. Uysal, *Kubad-Abad Sarayında Selçuklu Cam Sanatı.* Türk Tarih Kurumu Yayınları, Ankara 2013, see p. 112, figure.78 [for mouth of oil lamp with shade]; p. 128, figure. 90 [for window glass]; p. 92, figure. 59 [for bottle mouth]; p. 66, figure. 25-26, p. 68, figure. 30, p. 90, figure. 58 [for pedestals].
[73] For glass bracelets, see also. E. Eser, "Divriği Kalesi Yüzey Araştırması 2006", *25. Araştırma Sonuçları Toplantısı,* Vol. 3, Ankara 2008, p. 196, note 18.

Photo 83- Glass Bracelet Fragments

Bone objects; although a small number of objects were found, different objects such as knife handle, comb, reel, arrow ring, ring and beads were found. The knife handle (Photo 84) and the concentric circle motifs on the arrow ring are striking examples of quality workmanship.

Photo 84- Bone Knife Handle

Although the motif was widely used in the Early Christian period, it also appears in bone and ivory works from the early Islamic art. Combs, on the other hand (Photo 85), are examples of similar ones in Byzantine and Turkish-Islamic art, which continue to be produced in the same form today, with dense teeth on one side and sparse teeth on the other.

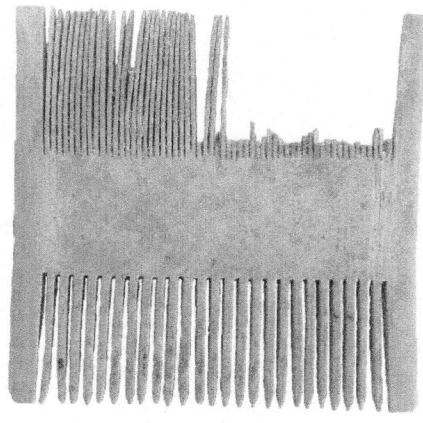

Photo 85- Bone Comb

Coins; it is one of the finding groups that has been extensively found during the excavations. The earliest identifiable example is a 6th century Byzantine coin. While the silver coin belonging to Kılıç Arslan II [1156-1192][74] (Photo 86) sheds light on the Seljuk period of the castle, many Ottoman coins found in the "Vaulted Space" near the south wall are important in terms of giving information about the late period of the castle.

Photo 86- Silver Coin, Kılıç Arslan II

---

[74] We would like to thank Mr. Gültekin Teoman, who warned us about the pronunciation of the aforementioned coin and provided us with the opportunity to make corrections, and Mr. Dr. Ahmet Özturhan, who examined the coin, for their interest and assistance. According to the examination, the Konya minted coin should belong to the first reign of I. Gıyaseddin Keyhüsrev and date back to either H. 593 or 595. Another person involved in this matter is Assoc. Prof. Dr. Mehmet Kutlu, and we also extend our heartfelt thanks to him for his valuable contributions.

6 EVALUATION

When the area is examined in general, it is approximately 400 m long and 200 m wide; It is located on rocky ground surrounded by water from the west, north and east.

It seems possible to group the analysis to be made in terms of settlement character under several headings due to the data received from the area.

Ceremonial Construction Period

The presence of blood pits and canals connecting to these pits, which are densely located at different places and heights, indicate the ceremonial character of the area. We think that the first settlement should be sought somewhere else rather than the castle area, because of these traces that are spread throughout the area and still continue to emerge during the works.

Necropolis Period

It is possible to define the second phase as the Necropolis Phase, based on the existence of burial chambers and grave niches as a development depending on the level of metal technology. Within the framework of what is known, it can be argued that this situation was established in the 1st century BC. The fact that the rock structure is very hard, especially in the section where the rock tomb chambers are located, must have been a result developed in parallel with the use of iron tools. It is considered that the number of four rock tomb chambers, two of which are open and the other two found as a result of excavation, will increase. Along with the burial chambers, there are also niches with different depths that were used for similar purposes. It does not seem possible today to know the exact date of the transition from the ceremony and sacrifice area to the grave area.

Warehouse-Outpost Period

Urartians are also mentioned in the history of the region. Considering the richness of the region in terms of iron ore, there is a possibility that Divriği could be an outpost and storage area in the hands of the Urartian's. Rock storage and cistern details can be counted among the architectural remains of this period. It is not possible to talk about any artifacts from this period, except for a similar piece unearthed in the Ayanis Castle. However, as the study progresses, the diversity of finds increases.

Rock Housing Period

We can argue that there was a phase in which burial chambers were used as residential areas. The increase in the number of warehouses and cisterns in each excavated region indicates that the number of people using the area had increased.

Wall Structure Period

It is currently not possible to know for certain when the first wall structure was built in the area. The only thing that can be said with certainty is that they have existed in the region since the beginning of the Byzantine domination. The fact that the materials found so far and dated to the Early Byzantine period are mostly coming from the upper section, leads us to think that the texture in this section mostly belongs to Byzantine Divriği. It is possible to focus on the fact that this section was surrounded by a wall and turned into a citadel after the 9th century, and that there was a wall settlement and texture that lasted at least two hundred years until the beginning of the Mengüjek days.

Turkish Period

We do not yet know the additions and changes that took place in the inner-city wall in the days when the Mengüjek process started. The first data in this area seems to be the construction of the two-phase Castle Mosque. The area to the south of the Castle Mosque, which is the most sheltered unit due to its location, should have been the area where the harem was placed. Although there are some researchers who tend to think that the Mengüjek palace is outside the area, the palace should be inside the inner castle due to its settlement character and period characteristics. There is a group of special artifacts discovered in this section.

The fact that the Castle Mosque has two phases, especially the windows in the south part of the eastern wall and the *mahfil* added in the second phase, which must have been a sultan's mahfil, necessitates the relevance of the building to the pre-Mengüjek period. On the subject, I suffice to say this much today.

Our most important expectation regarding the inner castle is the possibility of the emergence of a cleaning structure, namely a palace bath, as in many similar examples. The fact that the water tanks and snow wells feeding the lower parts of the castle are in this section is among the data that strengthens our expectation in this regard.

The most important Mengüjek operation in the area is the outer wall construction, the length of which exceeds 1000 meters. According to the inscriptions on it, the construction that started in the 1230s was completed in 1252. There are some interesting details regarding the exterior wall, which has been repaired in the last two years.

1- The construction started during the reign of Alaeddin Keykubad I. It is noteworthy that an outer wall was built in the Divriği Castle after Konya and Sivas against the Mongolian threat. It is highly probable that the request for the construction of the wall came from Konya. We will reiterate this issue later on.

2- The wall was built following a special method. Bastions and walls are not solid masses. They are built independently. Since it is an earthquake zone, such a special method must have been followed.
3- It has been stated before by Necdet Sakaoğlu that the architects who built the outer wall were the same people as those who built the Great Mosque, since the construction dates were parallel. This view is supported by the data from the field. The dilatation seen on the walls of the building ensemble also strengthens this view.
4- The suffix of the wall is the bastion, which is known as the Lion's Bastion with the inscription data on it and has a viewing terrace most probably associated with the palace spaces. There are lion statues sitting on the bastion, which is important because it overlooks both the great mosque and the city center. A similar use of figures is also seen on the outer wall, on the wall that curtains the gate, which we call the Sultan's Gate due to its location. Although there are some who stated that it was a bear figure in the past, it was understood that it was a lion relief, as a result of the cleaning and examination works that we carried out on the site. It was placed in its original place during the repair works.

It is suggested that there are a series of animal reliefs on this wall. Considering the Mengüjek practices, this is an acceptable view, but no data other than the aforementioned lion relief has been found yet. We follow the subject.

Mengüjek Applications on the Inner Wall

The data from the fields opened in this section are scarce but important. First of all, the burial chambers, wall niches and rock floor details that were previously shaped in this area were transformed into spaces with rubble stone walls and wooden ceilings built in front of them.

There are two different methods in wall material-technique. The first is the rubble stone-herringbone weave, which was used almost until the middle of the twentieth century. It can be seen on the walls of the castle mosque, as well as on the walls of the opened spaces. In this masonry technique, mud was used as the binding material.

Again, in the same area, two buildings, one to the east of the main gate and the other to the north, draw attention to their material-technical features. The binding material in both structures built with cut stone material is Khorasan mortar. It is highly probable that both buildings are private residences. One was described by us as a bathhouse and most likely had underfloor heating. In this regard, what is known about medieval Anatolian structures is quite limited. The possibility of the existence of other structures with similar systems at the same level seems to provide important information on this subject.

The Relationship between the Outer Wall and the Interior Area

Data has been followed up on this issue for a long time. So far, the data from both the Main Gate and the Sultan's Gate are not very promising. The expectation of a stone-paved road starting from the gates and extending into the area still continues, but there is no data. If the pavements belonging to such a road were not used in other places by being removed later, we can even say that the Mengüjeks did not even bother with the ground. The same is surprising in terms of wall quality. The outer wall seems to have been damaged since the time it was built. Maybe an earthquake took place which we have no information about.

7 CLOSING REMARKS

The Divriği Castle Excavation, that started with a surface survey in 2006 and turned into an excavation by the decision of the Council of Ministers in 2007, can be described as an excavation that has just begun.

The works in the inner wall area started in 2010.[75] While the studies were carried out in various parts of the area in the first eight years, the last seasons focused on the Cave Region.

As the studies progressed, the characteristic features of the area, both in terms of architecture and findings, began to appear gradually.

According to the data obtained from the areas introduced above, it has been understood that there has been great destruction over the centuries. The destruction is at a sad level both in terms of architectural data and small finds. Especially the spaces, which are understood to be covered with figured stucco decorated plates, are almost completely destroyed. In this sense, it is predicted that the data will increase in the coming seasons.

---

[75] As mentioned above, an excavation was carried out in 2009 in the study area of the same name with the aim of controlling the geophysical surveys.

Apart from stucco, there is also a large amount of data on other work groups. Extremely damaged artifacts form important traces of the rich life that once existed in Divriği Castle. It is possible to assume that the existing structures and spaces were repaired after the Turks came to the area. Traces of such repairs can still be seen on the intermediate wall. There is no historical data which shows that the city was conquered by the Turks as a war result, and there is no concrete data yet. Studies and evaluations on the subject are still ongoing.

As the Divriği Castle Excavation progresses and the underground parts continue to be unearthed, the traces of Mengüjek culture will be better read. Divriği Mengüjeks, who form an important branch of the Mengüjek family, will be able to be defined by their works and understanding of culture and art.

Our greatest wish is the continuation of the wall repair and the immediate implementation of the landscaping project.

ABOUT THE AUTHORS

Prof. Dr. Erdal Eser

The author, who is a faculty member at Sivas Cumhuriyet University, Faculty of Letters, Department of Art History, graduated from Hacettepe University, Faculty of Letters, Department of Archeology-Art History and completed his Master's and PhD at the same university. Erdal Eser has various studies published in his field.

Assoc. Prof. Meryem Acara Eser

The author, who is a faculty member at Sivas Cumhuriyet University, Faculty of Letters, Department of Art History, graduated from Hacettepe University, Faculty of Letters, Department of Archeology-Art History and completed her Master's and PhD at the same university. Byzantine Art expert, Assoc. Prof. Meryem Acara Eser has various studies published in her field.

Translated by:

Belgin Selen Haktanır and Ivana Mihaljinec, PhD

Editor: Ivana Mihaljinec, PhD

Made in the USA
Coppell, TX
20 September 2023